Sunlit Streams
of
Water

Devotions for Religious Naturalists

By

Erwin K. Thomas

Sunlit Streams of Water: Devotions for Religious Naturalists

Text copyright © 2020 by Erwin K. Thomas, Ph.D.

United States Copyright Office

Printed in the United States of America by Erwin K. Thomas, Ph.D.

Independent Publisher

First Paperback Edition: June 2020

ISBN – 13: 978-0-9966125-7-9

To my wife Mary, son Matthew, and
daughter-in-law Shannon

Other Works by Erwin K Thomas

Dfurstane's Spiritual Beliefs

Heaven Bound: Bread of Life

Guyana's Seawall Girl

Life's Passages: From Guyana to America

Gifts of God: Reflections & Affirmations

Keys of Faith: Fifty-Two Meditations for Living

A Weekly Encounter: Fifty-Two Meditations of Hope

Mass Media in 2025: Industries, Organizations, People, and Nations with Brown H. Carpenter

Handbook on Mass Media In The United States: The Industry and Its Audiences with Brown H. Carpenter

Make Better Videos with Your Camcorder

Contents

Introduction x

Belief in Religious Naturalism...xi

Part One: The Universal Spirit

The Soul of Eternal Spirit 2

Ode to Mother Nature...4

God Exists...5

A Prayer for Personal Guidance 7

God's Attributes 8

God's Creation 10

God in Nature 12

God's Abundant Blessings 14

God's Wisdom & Mercy...15

God's Precious Love..16

Marriage of Compatibility..18

Concepts of the Afterlife..20

Part Two: Objectives of Life

Stranger than Science Fiction...24

The Cycle of Life...26

Know Yourself 28

Nature & Nurture 30

The Truth About Life...32

Responsibility & Nature 34

The Storms of Life 36

Five Essentials of Life 38

The Essence of Life 39

Lives of Beauty...41

Living in God's Abundance...43

First, Do No Harm 45

Actions of Believers...47

Good & Bad Wildfires...49

Time & Money 51

Climb that Mountain...53

Holy, but Dirty Water...55

The Meaning of Life...57

Part Three: Noteworthy Celebrations

Commonalities of Religions...60

With Light There's Illumination...61

Aloe Vera – God's Angel 63

The Beauty of Black-Eyed Susan...65

Birth, Death, & Consciousness..67

Valentine's Day 69

Happy Birthday..70

50th Wedding Anniversary 72

Streams of Love 74

Miracles of Summer 76

Mother's Day Prayer 78

Father's Day Prayer 80

On Labor Day 82

Joys of Christmas..84

The Miracle of Life 86

Juneteenth Freedom Day..88

Independence Day (U.S.A)..90

Part Four: Social Goals

Acting with Actors..94

Pursue Higher Goals 96

Leaders' Role 98

Journey in Life 100

Be a Gift-Giver 102

Live How You Like 104

World Day of Prayer 106

Women in Society 108

Reusable Bags & Totes...110

Streams of Consciousness 111

Be Wise about Power 113

Limitations of Prayer 115

The Sacred Elephant 117

Quest for Purity 119

Celebration of Wicca/Pagan Litha Yule...........................121

Part Five: Hope in Suffering

Life Is Beautiful 124

A Therapy Pet 126

The Good in Suffering 127

Good & Bad Luck 129

Make Lemonade...131

A Balanced Life 133

God/Nature Fights Back...135

Healing in Life 137

Partition Guyana? 139

LGBTQIA 141

With Tears Help Us God! 143

A Pandemic Is Deadly..145

Chance: Key to Crisis 147

Dove of Healing..149

Christ Is Risen! 151

In Honor of Service Men and Women..153

National Symbolism in Fire...154

Selected Bibliography 156

Appendix A 160

Appendix B..163

About the Author..165

Introduction

Sunlit Streams of Water: Devotions for Religious Naturalists conjure up diverse and tantalizing symbols. This book of poetic devotions attempts to capture the symbolism of "sunlight," "streams," and "water." Its themes represent the life, energy, power, and rebirth depicted in the sun. Sunlight appears as the completion of God's great work. An illuminated stream shows the passage of time. Movement of the bodies of water demonstrates the beginning of life as it flows into the vast oceans of the earth. This symbolism shows a pathway to our hearts and a descent to the primitive nature of humanity, but water itself represents birth, fertility, and refreshment. It's a symbol of life itself. In instances, it could be construed as negative and uncertain. So although water is used for purification and healing, it has overtones of suffering and redemption. In Christianity it's the symbol of baptism, while the Holy Spirit is depicted as celestial fire. But for the religious naturalist God isn't anthropomorphic, but is in with nature's manifestations.

Part One: The Universal Spirit glorifies the attributes of God.

Part Two: Objectives of Life examines the nature and meaning of life.

Part Three: Noteworthy Celebrations captures aspects of life's experiences.

Part Four: Social Goals reveals aspects of people's earthly journey.

Part Five: Hope in Suffering explains ways of dealing with sorrow and other unexpected problems.

Belief in Religious Naturalism

The author's beliefs are a testimony to Transcendentalism with a faith in nature. In this treatise nature is paramount in people's lives. Natural phenomena always play a vital role. Every aspect of nature is important to mankind's thinking and actions. Our mind, body, and soul are guided by nature. People shouldn't make the mistake of thinking that nature was separate from them, for they are intricately interrelated with its soul. Nature's beauty is blended with all natural gifts. "Nature is all in all" and embraces every aspect of life.

To embrace the all in all is having an appreciation of the Creator's manifestations. The heavenly bodies - the sun, moon, and stars, known and unknown planets traversing the sky are phenomenal. The trees, plants, oceans, rivers, streams, mountains, hills and valleys speak in their own language while buffeted by the wind. So are the seasons – spring, summer, autumn, and winter with their distinct moods. Sometimes it's calm, beautiful, and glorious. Occasionally there are hurricanes, earthquakes, tsunamis, floods, and forest fires.

But birds, reptiles, fishes, and animals of all sorts inhabit the earth living in the air, land, or sea. They breed, feed, and exist in an unpredictable reality. These creatures are provided for by nature. People breathe fresh air, pick fruits, feast on delicious foods, drink refreshing water, build cozy houses from trees, light fires to cook meals, and dress warmly in winter months with nature's bounty.

These manifestations are only a part of the Eternal Essence that's within, above, below, and around us. To personalize such an Essence is only a metaphor. S/he is omniscient, omnipresent, omnipotent, immanent, and transcendent. No words could adequately describe the sum of this all-encompassing Reality.

Erwin K. Thomas, Ph.D.

PART ONE: THE UNIVERSAL SPIRIT

The Soul of Eternal Spirit

Sitting on the porch watching the world go by

Lots of familiar things I didn't notice before

Large rocks just lounging around

With leaves on trees fluttering in the breeze

And geese in pairs strolling idly by

But what delighted me most

Was how majestic everything looked

A mild wind blew intermittently

Birds on tree tops chirped melodiously

And flowering plants enjoyed the spectacle

Across the way stood a sparkling lake

And the street reflected the summer heat

But today no neighbors were mulling around

This was the true Essence of Life

Just the Universal Spirit gluing everything together

Although the huge brown rocks stood still

As the branches of trees swayed in the breeze

With an occasional car passing by

This Divine Presence could clearly be felt

Yes! And it had a message,

"My Presence isn't a person – man, woman, or child.

It's the Soul of Eternal Spirit."

"Universal Spirit, thank you for the inspiration for I was able to recognize the Divine in nature."

Amen

Ode to Mother Nature

I praise nature as the Primordial Reality with all its phenomena.

I acclaim and delight in nature's abundance with all things in the Universe.

I need and embrace fully the ecstatic joy in all of nature's diversity.

I think and reflect on the splendor of all species on planet earth.

I honor the heart and mind by living in sync with nature's majesty.

I easily and methodically walk through the world's gardens of nature's landscape.

I insist that nature's beauty would captivate lovers to embrace its delights with their souls.

I see clearly nature's glory in the night sky, on green land, and while sailing the seas.

I take deep breaths to welcome nature's splendor that's there to greet us daily.

God Exists

It's a mistake to only imagine God.

Therefore God is real.

He exists.

The universe had to start from somewhere.

So God always had to be around.

Everything in the world has limits.

And there's always a cause and effect.

But there must be God who was before everything else.

God is infinite.

Let's take a look at nature.

Every element is in a specific order.

The sun, moon, and stars radiate light.

People know night and day.

Trees blossom during their appointed season.

Such a complex order requires a Creator.

So God exists.

Most people have morals.

They inherently have a sense of what's right and wrong.

Humankind won't arbitrarily commit murder.

They live according to the laws.

It's God alone who makes moral requirements valid.

God's the absolute lawgiver.

Therefore God exists.

"Eternal Essence let us rejoice in the inherent gifts of the Universe. Through these masterpieces people are assured of your existence."

Amen

A Prayer for Personal Guidance

Holy God let me see what I should see.

Unchangeable God let me say what I should say.

Truthful God let me hear what I should hear.

Precious God let me smell what I should smell.

Infinite God let me touch what I should touch.

Wise God let me sense what I should sense.

Creator God let me discern what I should discern.

Omniscient God let me know what I should know.

Spiritual God let me be what I should be.

Gracious God let me think what I should think.

Sustainer God let me walk where I should walk.

Eternal God let me go where I should go.

Omnipotent God let me become what I should become.

Omnipresent God I thank you for guiding me.

Amen

God's Attributes

God has glorious attributes

And with his saints there's extreme joy

They experience happiness in striving for perfection.

Happiness from God

Is like a flame enlightening our lives

Believers find bliss in the Holy Spirit.

This gift of Spirit is symbolic

Of the Divine's transcendent glory,

God's image is beyond created wisdom,

As the Creator of the Universe

God is the Father of Abraham, Isaac, and Jacob.

He provides us with our earthly homes.

And we dwell in the worldly paradise

Exalting our minds and bodies

With such blessings believers live in bliss.

As blessed beings we strive for eternal rest.

After departing our earthly domain

In Spirit we'll praise him.

Hunger and thirst will be no more.

For in heaven there'll be the ultimate reality

That people will encounter

So continue to walk as spirit-filled beings

Follow your bliss

And the universe will open doors

Where there are walls

This is our ultimate journey,

For nothing is impossible with God

*"Divine Essence, help us to have greater insights into your attributes.
Guide us in our quest to discover the ultimate reality of life."*

Amen

God's Creation

How do people make sense of God's Creation?

God's manifestations of the celestial sky, rotating earth, far-flung
  lands,

Mountains, rivers, animals, flora, and fauna

Grace us every day and night

But it's through our senses people delight in these phenomena.

Scientists verify the modulations of the rising and setting sun.

People note the changes to the earth when it heats up and cools down.

That's how we know what to expect in every season of the year.

Science tells us of impending storms and natural disasters.

It's this understanding that determines the facts of life

But it isn't only people's understanding at work.

They have to rely on their intuition to make a necessary leap.

In fully understand the workings of the Divine

This creative process leads to formal proof

And makes it possible for us to set goals, have beliefs, and attitudes
  about the Universe

Over centuries scientific research has developed

And answered questions concerning beliefs in the sacred books

So people now understand why different cultures might have divergent beliefs about faith and morality

"Eternal Spirit, help us to find the true nature of reality.
Guide us in our understanding to have better perspectives about the faith
traditions of the world."

Amen

God in Nature

What causes lightning to strike?

What brings thunderstorms?

Lightning flashes when positively

And negatively charged particles interact

Grow large enough to form a giant spark

But thunderstorms form from an unstable air mass

When warm and usually cold air collide

Yet some sacred texts show this is how God speaks

God might explodes, brings judgment, and condemn

But how did the ancients believe these were acts of God?

Scientists, prophets, theologians tend to agree

That there must be "cause and effect"

So they determine God possesses this power

Because the Eternal Spirit exists in nature

Other phenomena are just as revealing

Tsunamis are sudden movement of the ocean because of
earthquakes,

Volcanoes are formed from the buoyancy of the magma,

And pressure from absolved gases,

Hurricanes are due to intense low pressure areas

That forms in the summer or fall over warm waters

"God, help us to be cognizant of nature's phenomena. Why these manifestations often cause devastations are based on mysteries of your omniscience. Protect us from the storms of life."

Amen

God's Abundant Blessings

God – Please listen to my prayer.

God – Thank you for waking me up on this glorious day.

God – Guide me safely all day long.

God – Help me to do always what's right in your sight.

God – And when I fall pick me to get up again.

God – Be with my loved ones - family, neighbors, and friends.

God – Protect us as we go about our daily lives.

God – We thank you for this season of the year.

God – We love the glittering stars, moonlit nights, and rays of sunlight.

God – Nor must we forget the gentle breeze that sweeps across the countryside.

God – It's the air we breathe that gives everything life.

God – Let us meditate in our hearts on our wonderful gifts.

God – For it's through your grace we're alive and well.

God – I thank you from the bottom of my heart for these abundant blessings.

Amen

God's Wisdom & Mercy

God's wisdom and mercy are indescribable

For the Divine is known for infinite grace

Christian believers have an apostolic Spirit

They embrace this eternal gift for spiritual growth

That's seen as an unquenchable fire

A devotee of this Universal Essence says,

"Don't go where the path may lead,

But go instead where there's no path

And be sure to leave a trail."

Contemplating God is great

For people experience goodness and mercy

Love heals wounded hearts

So when you witness think about God's omnipotence

For this is how to touch unfaithful people

In your pastoral outreach love all mankind

Be industrious and walk in the light

And be devoted believers of the Word

For its God's wisdom

"Almighty God, grant us the peace that passes all understanding. Let our words be soothing to all we encounter on our earthly sojourn."

Amen

God's Precious Love

Sowing love brings joy to precious hearts

When people receive the fruits of God's grace

These gifts sustain their souls

Causing them to rejoice in the Spirit

Love isn't about good people getting better

It's about the good news of bad people

Coping with their failures

For most have fallen short of God's gracious love

And it's through Divine's redemption they are made whole

People ought to love their neighbors like themselves

By sharing warmth and tenderness

It's God's love that blossoms in us

Like new petals after a rainstorm

But these gifts have to be nurtured

For its through believers people know God's beauty

Beyond comparison is proclaiming God's love

That's planted deeply within people's hearts

And their joy springs like flowers in springtime

How great is God in a believer's life!

The Divine always shows love in the world.

"Divine Essence, you touch many lives. Help us to grow and blossom like flowers in springtime."

Amen

Marriage of Compatibility

Nature is predictable and unpredictable.

That's the way of its laws.

So the Law of Attraction is just the same.

People say, "Opposites attract."

That's true and false.

With subatomic particles of positive protons

And negative neutrons that's always true

Christians intermarry believers of other faiths –

Jews, Chinese, Japanese, Africans, Hindus, Buddhists, and Muslims

Whites marry Blacks; Blacks are marrying Asians, and Asians, Native Americans

Many of these unions last a life time.

People also say, "Like attracts like."

Again we are witnessing Christians intermarrying same-sex believers.

LGBTQ+ has gained national prominence.

Males are marrying males, females marrying females, and bisexuals marrying bisexuals

These individuals are from different faiths, and some might be nonbelievers

Believers ask the question, "Why is it that life is this way?"

But the truth is life is consistent and inconsistent.

The Universal Spirit is at work when males marry females, and
believers' nonbelievers.

*"Supreme Spirit, grant us the insight to understand the diversity of your
manifestations. Let us see that positives don't always attract negatives
and vice versa. But you have shown us that people marry because of their
compatibility."*

Amen

Concepts of the Afterlife

In World Religions and Beliefs

And its concepts of the Afterlife

Are diverse

And shrouded in mystery

Every faith has its own beliefs

That range from bodily resurrection,

The survival of the soul, judgment,

Merging of consciousness,

Heaven and hell, reincarnation

Of animals, insects, and plants;

Moksha, or salvation in Hinduism,

Enlightenment, and nirvana in Buddhism

The Abrahamic religions – Judaism, Christianity,

And Islam believe in the resurrection,

Judgment, heaven, and hell;

While the Indian faiths –

Buddhism, Hinduism, Jainism,

And Sikhism believe in karma,

Some form of rebirth,

Or transmigration as the Samara doctrine

Of the cycle of life and death

"Primal Essence, enable us to grasp the mysteries of the Afterlife. Help us to understand more fully its many beliefs."

Amen

PART TWO:
OBJECTIVES OF LIFE

Stranger than Science Fiction

What? When? Where? How? Why?

At times don't apply to science

How the universe originated?

From an infinitesimal speck boggles the mind

How did this speck cause the Big Bang?

Is hard to comprehend,

But it's a scientific explanation of how the universe originated

Why the universe is teeming with planets and black holes?

Raises many questions

If an astrophysicist could conceivably place a clock

In the center of a black hole, time would slow until the clock
stops

Still the universe is governed by laws – there's gravitation, matter,
energy,

And infinite space in the ever-expanding galaxies

Life originated from a primordial sea from nonliving entities,

But still a scientist is unable to duplicate this phenomenon in the
lab

Albert Einstein proved that matter and energy are similar

The atheist Stephen Hawing wrote if there was a God

He would be impersonal, and be in the laws of nature

But this would be a definition – not a fact.

*"God, give us wisdom in understanding the mysteries of the universe.
But help us to be cognizant that when some mysteries are revealed there
would be other profound ones to understand."*

Amen

The Cycle of Life

The human cycle of life has stages

Childhood, adolescence, and adulthood

Are a part of this development

Life begins with a pregnancy

With a birth of immense potential

Parents are the caregivers

That raise their children with hope

The childhood years are filled with imagination.

It's a time of exploration and transformation.

Children learn social skills

And are groomed to take on life's responsibilities

The adolescent years are a time of puberty

There are changes in their bodies

But in the adult years people find mates,

Get a job, make a home, and raise a family

Once matured families have grown

People are wiser, benevolent,

And have a rich repository of knowledge

Later adulthood is a time of reflection

People are living life to the fullest

So when parents die,

A legacy passes down from generation to generation

"Divine Maker, help us to live our life to the fullest. Guide us during our earthly sojourn, and help us to live in peace."

Amen

Know Yourself

You're a Mini-universe

Living with trillions of Universes

In a macro-world

You're a thinking, breathing

And an imaginative being

Only God knows who you really are!

What people see isn't the real you.

You're constantly evolving

By taking on new forms

Much of what people see is on the surface

But hidden from view

Is your true self, thoughts, and perceptions

Of your personality

This is your image to the world

To all hidden Universes

You have an identity

Your behavior is in certain ways

But you're like a mask

In this whole intricate Universe

To all those people

Who believe they know you

Socrates said, "Philosopher, know thyself!"

"Almighty Creator, grant us the wisdom to know ourselves. Give us the insights to be accountable for what we do, and be transparent."

Amen

Nature & Nurture

Nature and nurture go hand in hand
Although they are uniquely different
Nature is in our genes
We're born that way
With certain physical and personality traits
Irrespective where people were raised

What a person inherits biologically from their parents
From their childhood can't be changed in any way
But nurture is through the environment in which we live
And this can be modified for the better
It helps when children are raised by loving parents.

As people grow their health is nurtured in many ways
This could be through their diet
Their amount and type of exercise
How they sleep
And the type of work they do

Where people live is important
Are they from an urban environment?
With skyscrapers, traffic congestion, and pollution

Or do they live in the country?

Where there are open spaces, trees, lakes, mountains, and fresh air

The results of living under these conditions play a major role in shaping their lives.

"Eternal Spirit, help us make good choices concerning how, and where we live. Guide us in cultivating a healthy lifestyle."

Amen

The Truth About Life

Layers of rocks reveal stories of our past

They are like books to be read

With leaves that show how life evolved

Still some well-known people

Have doubts about mankind's beginnings

Christians might hold the story in Genesis to be true

Concerning how God created mankind

And they like to tell the tale of Adam and Eve

About how God took a rib from Adam to create Eve

But does this make sense or isn't it a myth?

Scientists tell us a different story

They have revealed that over thousands of years life forms
evolved

And this seems to be no surprise

Since all beings and nonbeings are intricately interrelated

So many Bible stories are nothing more than myths

Yet creationists believe in the literal meaning of Scripture

Knowing the truth about religious texts is important

Scripture was written ages ago

When belief systems were embryonic

So it'll take the empiricists' and rationalists' thinkers to make sense
   of life

*"Divine Nature, open our eyes and help us see clearly what's right.
Give us the insight to decipher what's true. And help us in our quest in
understanding the mysteries of the Universe."*

Amen

Responsibility & Nature

Responsibility to nature calls for discipline.

As we grow up people traverse the stages of life.

They are buffeted by the winds of change.

Some of their experiences are good, while others are bad.

But it takes discipline to put life's vicissitudes into perspective.

What do people do when they are knocked down?

It's best to jump up again and fight.

What do people do when the going is rough?

It's good to keep plugging along.

Nothing in life is easy, but problems test our will.

It's good to be disciplined and able to withstand assaults.

It's a sign of maturity when people don't overdo.

Like Buddhism it's best to live in moderation.

Watch what you eat and drink.

Make sure you meditate and exercise every day.

Be good to others as you'll like them to be good to you.

Make friends and be benevolent to those you meet.

Let the natural processes of life guide you.

Enjoy the beauty of the sun, moon, and stars.

Let the wind caress your face.

Watch the trees dance across the landscape.

And plunge in the ocean of life, and splash in the waves.

*"Eternal Essence, guide us to embrace life's vicissitudes.
Let us be open to nature's promptings, and be filled with serenity."*

Amen

The Storms of Life

Some things are the way they are

And can't be changed

People pray that they will remain the same

While there are those things

That can be changed

And it's for us to know the difference

We know what the unchangeable things are

Day and night

Birth and death

Seasons come and go

There are the changing elements of wind, water, and fire

The Universe presents its many manifestations

With an abundance of life forms

Praising the sun, moon, oceans, mountains, and valleys

But these revelations from Our Creator are forever changing

They appear and disappear with sometimes disastrous effects

Some rivers rise and fall overflowing their banks bringing death and
    havoc.

Volcanic mountains erupt that decimate communities and villages

Lightning causes forest fires and devastation of trees worldwide

And mankind is impacted by earthquakes, monsoons, hurricanes, and tsunamis

That devastated millions of people's lives causing death, suffering, and destruction

However believers pray to their deity or deities with these impending catastrophes

That these calamities would pass us by without harm

"Universal Spirit, help us concerning how we face the storms of life. Guide us safely through these disasters."

Amen

Five Essentials of Life

One – The Word is the Universal Spirit
Causing everything to exist
And this Word forms the basis
Of the world's religions

Two – The breath or wind is of God,
Making it possible for us to be alive

Three – The sun is like a ball of fire
Suppling energy, evaporating water,
Determining the seasons,
And causing storms on the earth

Four – The earth consists of matter
Through which all animate
And inanimate things are composed

Five – All matter consists of water.
Oceans, rivers, and streams
Are replenished by the rains and snowstorms
From the heavens above

"Gracious Provider, help us to appreciate these gifts to mankind. Guide us to use your blessings wisely."

Amen

The Essence of Life

I often dream about change.

These experiences come and go.

Some are quite pleasant.

But one thing seems certain

Change is the Essence of Life.

In the beginning people didn't know

From whence they came

Who would be their parents?

Yet they became gifts to the world,

As blessings in their beloved country

They arrived with a mission in mind

Imagine people were once embryos,

A bundle of interacting cells,

And with the changes that occurred

They grew into be adults

Yes! These changes were miraculous

All designed with a divine purpose

People were once kids beaming with joy,

They experienced changes in their adolescent years,

But were taught what was right and wrong

And grew to be adults in special vocations

Becoming models to their society

People experienced life's changes

That hit them straight between the eyes

Yet these realities molded them

And shaped them to be who they really are

Weren't these changes that graced their lives?

Making them the best that nature has to offer

"God with your blessings the Eternal Spirit has shaped us to be models in the world. Guide us to be perfect channels in our communities."

Amen

Lives of Beauty

This is a world of beauty

When love is all around us

On sunlit days strolling along the beach

We're greeted with crushing waves

In winter, just glancing at the ice-covered mountains

Gracing the skyline is delightful

But in our daily lives

There exist other beauties

We encounter these gifts

On our journey through life

These are the people we love

That touches us in joyful ways

We're attracted to their smiles, laughter,

And personal qualities

They are members of families, neighbors, and friends

That are all reaching out to us

And their gifts are the cornerstone of our lives

Beauty surrounds them

That we're blessed to enjoy

They are honest and lovely people

And this is the first chapter of wisdom

This truth they have captured

In well-lived lives

"Loving God, help us to be cognizant of such people in our lives. Grant that we are able to be models of their benevolent blessings."

Amen

Living in God's Abundance

Living in God's abundance brings blessings.

This means not being self-centered.

One test is by providing enough

To those who don't have much

Abundance might come with material wealth

But be sure to opt for peace, contentment,

Grace and humility

And accept such gifts with an open heart

Often people pray when faced with challenges

They do so when distressed and in need.

But embrace joy in your abundance.

For these gifts thank God!

People must love what they do

They must be enthused in spreading happiness

Doing what they love is the cornerstone

For having abundance in life

But please don't clamor for wealth

If God gives you the world's goods

They are to help you gain insight

To be a good example to mankind

For everything depends on how you use your treasure

Your gifts ought to be instruments of blessing

For this is the way to live with wealth

"Divine Essence, show us the true way to live with our gifts.
If it is wealth let us be, a blessing to others."

Amen

First, Do No Harm

"Primum non nocere"

Is the Latin translation from the original Greek

For the oath, "First, do no harm."

It's the Hippocratic Oath that medical students take.

But it's also the tenets enshrined

In the world's religions of Jainism, Hinduism, and Buddhism

Doctors will undoubtedly do harm

As they attempt to treat patients

How could they not order tests? CT scans,

MRIs, mammograms, biopsies, and vaccinations

These procedures could have harmful effects.

But doctors have to recommend them

Because the potential benefits outweigh the risks.

But religious faith traditions like Jainism, Hinduism,

And Buddhism have principles of nonviolence

For these faiths the concept of "do no harm"

Not only extends to all living organisms

But how believers think about words and deeds

For believers hold that thoughts are important

In the way they live their lives

Actions of Believers

Put love into practice by serving mankind.

This calls for having humble hearts

And a positive outlook

Such love has to be authentic

That demonstrates a loving God

The Divine has a special place in our lives

For the poor, needy, and prisoners

By loving our rejected brothers and sisters

We focus on the Eternal Essence's promises

That's alive within us

The ultimate tragedy in life

Isn't the oppression and cruelty of the weak?

But the silence of good people

About such bad deeds

Rejected people are God's gifts to us

As we are to them

Loving them should be universal

This is a sublime connectedness

And believers support this truth when they step forward

To play their part in their communities

Where they live

Goodness is created and recreated

It is nurtured into amazing realities

When a believer's actions become Holy

Expressing the eternal blessings of our Creator

"Eternal Essence, help us to promote what's good and just in life. Teach us to recognize that all citizens – rich and poor alike, have inevitable rights."

Amen

Good & Bad Wildfires

Wildfires could occur in any place

In the United States, Canada, Australia,

And even the Western Cape of South Africa

Natural fires generally start by lightning.

Some are by spontaneous combustion of sawdust and dried leaves

And human-caused wildfires are caused by a number of other reasons

Still there are good and bad forest fires

They are bad when they destroy homes

Causing a loss of lives and millions of acres

Wildlife suffers and many species are wiped out

But such fires also kill trees that prevent erosion

Having a negative impact on the environment

But wildfires are good when they are beneficial

These fires turn dead trees of the forest, and decaying plant matter into ashes

Causing nutrients to return to the soil instead of being trapped in dead plant vegetation

So wildfires clear the decaying trees of debris while returning health to the forest

And some plants depend on the heat to help them germinate

In forests more trees die because of insect infestation and disease than
from fires

So nature is both good and bad, for fires help restore the forests'
ecosystem

And decomposed organic matter enriches the soil with minerals, and
new plant grow

*"Eternal Essence you have shown that from bad there could be good.
So help us to have a better knowledge of nature."*

Amen

Time & Money

Time is like money

And has to be spent wisely

So why let people waste your time?

It's also tricky but can be used for good

In short, time is more than money.

To God, "A thousand years are like one day."

But a lifetime for a human is like a grain of sand

Still people are blessed with wonderful gifts

These qualities they share with God's creation.

Time is necessary for growth and development.

Over a period all organisms must have nutrients to grow

With years of education people learn lessons for life

Believers are fed spiritual food

To develop qualities of hope, faith, and love

With time dreams become realities

Workers may ask, "Do I have what it takes to do a job?

Is my ability suitable for a certain career?

Or am I sincere about my aptitude?"

Before endeavoring to undertake their life's mission

But living is a challenge

And as people undertake tasks

They must take breaks for rejuvenation

For life isn't only for fun times

It's for doing God's work

But whatever people do

It's best to aim for a well-balanced life.

"Eternal Spirit, help us to use time wisely. Guide us to make the best use of our gifts to live a well-balanced life."

Amen

Climb that Mountain

Climb that mountain

God has set before you

Your goal is to reach the summit

So don't remain stuck in a valley

But discover your purpose in life

You mustn't be lukewarm pursuing your goal

But be passionate about it

Give it the best shot discovering who you are

Is your purpose loving your family?

Then love your husband, wife, and kids

With one's whole heart, body, and soul

Show them you care by what you do

Just don't say the word 'love'

But act and be passionate about it.

Is your purpose promoting humanity?

Then bless those you encounter

Make friends with those on the highways and byways

Give generously to the poor, hungry, and destitute

And affirm your passion for mankind

Is your passion in a career?

If you teach be the best teacher of your students

If you're in sports be a credit to the team

If you're a writer explore stories that build up readers

If you're a scientist do research to improve patients' health

And if you're a religious, pray for, and with the world, for God's creation

For when you find your purpose, you'll be a role model.

"Gracious Spirit, help us to be the best that we can. Show us where we fit in God's scheme of things."

Amen

Holy, but Dirty Water

Holy, but dirty water might kill religious believers

When they emerge themselves

In the Jordan River to be baptized

Or, take a dip in the Ganges River

As part of their ceremonial rite

Many people might be unaware

That these waters are polluted

They are filled with human waste, and chemicals

From agricultural and industrial products

This is the case of the Jordan River

That flows southward through northern Israel

Where Jesus Christ was baptized by John the Baptist

The same is true for India's Ganges River

That flows from the Himalayas

Where there's raw sewage,

And remains of cremated corpses,

Chemical dyes from tanneries,

And animal carcasses

Yet Hindus fulfill their religious duties

For ritual purity, by emerging themselves in these waters

Infectious diseases could be spread

Through such contaminated waters

Like typhoid, cholera, paratyphoid fever,

Dysentery, jaundice, and malaria,

By chemicals, pesticides, nitrates, lead, and arsenic

These pollutants are all dangerous

To our nervous system and could even cause cancer

"Eternal One, help believers to be wise by safeguarding their health for God might bless them, but not prevent illness, or death."

Amen

The Meaning of Life

Let the mountains roar

Let peace reign

Let blessings pour from the sky

Like an abundant rainfall in summer

But what does this mean?

Our Eternal Spirit is the One

Who feeds the children of every race, color, and creed

Like the lilies and birds of field

Wherever they live on planet earth

Whether in bramble huts, simple homes, or extravagant palaces

But what does this mean?

This Universal Spirit is Our Provider

Who knows each little breath we take

As we work at simple and great tasks –

True manifestations of our natural gifts

With which God has endowed us

But what does this mean?

The Almighty One sustains us

Lifts us up when we slumber

And once aroused we venture into the world

To make our mark in Our Earthly Home

But what does this mean?

With these special gifts

As people of different faiths

Christians, Jews, Muslims, Hindus, and Atheists

All seeking answers to the Universe's Big Question:

"What is the meaning of life?"

And still many don't know the answer.

"Universal Essence, you have blessed us with many gifts, but still people aren't sure about the meaning of life. Shouldn't people embrace their gifts to find happiness and fulfillment in their lives?

Amen

PART THREE: NOTEWORTHY CELEBRATIONS

Commonalities of Religions

Most major religions have a doctrine

A set of principles and teachings

And stories based on myths

About gods and spiritual events

These faith traditions focus on experiences

Describing what their followers ponder in sacred texts

About God, gods, angels, or other Divine beings

Believers are known for their places of worship

Whether in a Church, Temple, or Synagogue

Where activities are coordinated

Religious leaders provide instructions

About how believers should live holy lives

And ways for its members to practice their faith

Members follow rituals of spiritual significance

Often with prayer, fasting, and feasts

But religious holidays are for festivals

Where there are blessings of deities

And celebrating the lives of saints and gurus

"Divine Providence, let us embrace the underlying teachings of religion – of love and mindfulness. Help us to respect all faith traditions, and realize there are different ways to encounter God."

Amen

With Light There's Illumination

With revelation deities and saints show goodness, clarity, and insight

Light is also a symbol of purity

Buddhist's and Bodhisattva's light come from within.

Often it's depicted as a rainbow or flame above their heads

Showing that they have achieved Enlightenment

In Hinduism light symbolizes Brahman – the eye, self, gods, and divinity.

Believers see this as the power of the sun, a star, or planet.

Often it's an illumination of the mind – brilliance, happiness, and prosperity.

Devout Hindus are inspired by wisdom, knowledge, intuition, and energy.

In Christianity light is a motif that resides within.

The minds of faithful Christians are considered enlightened.

This act is considered supernatural, and part of their religious life from creation.

Believers hold that with light dark deeds would dissipate.

Christians are taught to view themselves as the light of the world.

By so doing the Angles of Light would work on their behalf.

Sikhs and Quakers also have a concept of inner light.

But all believers are blessed with the light of stars twinkling on moonlit nights.

Many see the light shining brightly revealing the truth of love.

Light is an instrument of peace.

Most believers are blessed with the light of courage.

For Christians, the Prince of Peace is a Savior, Teacher, Guardian, Provider, and Flame of Hope.

"Divine Teacher, with light let all believers help heal the brokenhearted of the world by praying for peace, love, and truth."

Amen

Aloe Vera – God's Angel

O behold the green aloe with succulent stems

It's a Godsend

And people see this plant as an angel

Strangers – ordinary folk, gardeners,

And farmers do their part to grow this plant

They are sure to care and nurture it in the right way

And that's the love they share with this plant

Aloe Vera must be watered infrequently to discourage rot

So its caretakers have to be certain the soil is dry before watering it

The aloe needs six to eight hours of direct sunlight daily

And there must be sandy soil if the plant is grown in- or outdoors

If the tips of the aloes become brown

It's a problem with too much watering

This plant even grows well indoors with indirect sunlight

But still gardeners must check the soil

And remove roots that rot

Aloe Vera is an angel for its life-generating properties

And it's a popular ingredient in Indian and South Asian dishes

It can be eaten cooked or raw

But what else is this plant good for?

For centuries it has been used as a tropical skin cream

It's a laxative that helps with constipation.

The "meat" inside its leaves is used for treating skin conditions such
as psoriasis

And aloe creams have a calming effect by reducing itchiness, and
inflammation of the skin

*"Eternal Essence Thank you for Aloe Vera – the flourishing angelic plant
that provides us with health benefits."*

Amen

The Beauty of Black-Eyed Susan

Yes! People are more than humans

They are helpers of nature

We're able to make plants grow

And we're active participants in the process

But it's the Universal Spirit that determines the outcome.

Take black-eyed Susan

There's a planter's playbook to get the best results.

Black-eyed Susan must be planted

When the soil temperature is around 70 degrees

For best germination of its seeds

The planting period is from March to May

These seedlings will flower from June to September.

The black-eyed Susan enjoys the sun

So be sure to give them plenty sunlight

But be mindful and fertilize the soil for best results

Check the plants regularly so see if they need watering

And be sure they don't dry out

Further tips would have a gardener remove faded or dead leaves to
    prolong blooming

Knowing when to prune so that smaller blooms might occur in
the fall

But everything we do we're just helping nature

To ensure that the black-eyed Susan grows their best

Still a gardener has to guard against slugs, snails, Aphids,

And fungi by using an organic and antifungal program

*"Universal Spirit, you have graced us with the beautiful black-eyed
Susan. Help us to care for their growth successfully by passing on healthy
traits from generation to generation. For it does only through nature all
plants grow."*

Birth, Death, & Consciousness

Just imagine life begins with a sperm and an egg

Multiple choices become apparent

But all results favor only one combination

It's amazing how people come to be

But when was our true beginning?

Life originated through the Universal Essence

That's how everything eventually took form

From this point all living beings began

And religions paint multifaceted pictures of this account

But which faith gives the best account?

In the West and the East beliefs differ

And are based on religion and science

Science has defined birth and death

From the sperm and egg to the absence of brain waves

But when does life begin and end?

In Christianity Mary was overshadowed by the Holy Spirit

And was able to conceive the Savior Jesus Christ

While in the East Hinduism and Buddhism

Based their teachings on reincarnation,

Living with the concept of birth and rebirth

But it appears everything originates from Spirit

Matter is never destroyed but recycled

So all livings things end up at death as One Reality

And being part of the cycle of the Universal Essence

In the end all living things will merge into Oneness

To be a collective consciousness with the Universal Essence

*"Universal Spirit, help us to understand about birth and death.
Let us be cognizant of how creation unfolds."*

Amen

Valentine's Day

Not too often there's a day when so much love is spread.

Today is such a day!

It's a day for caring and being cared for.

It's a day of joy as we embrace everyone we love.

I extend this love to my family, friends,

Colleagues, the humble, and weak

Thanking them for the good things they do

Thanking them for making the earth safer

Thanking them for their efforts to bring joy to the world

Thanking them for their sacrifices that often go unnoticed

Thanking them for being true to themselves

When the going gets tough

"Eternal Essence, I especially like to thank you for the many people meet in their daily lives. Help us that they will be a positive influence."

Amen

Happy Birthday

What a special day!

To celebrate my birthday

So I kick back and relax

And take a toast

For it's the day of my birth

"Congratulations!" I said,

"I've made it another year."

I rang bells,

"Praise God I'm alive and well!"

Roll in the birthday cake

Let friends gather around

Light the candles

And I'll make a wish

For it's a time to celebrate

God has been good to me.

Pour the Burgundy

Let all raise their glasses,

"To a long life and a prosperous year!"

I blew out the candles

And made a wish,

"May all be blessed on this special day!"

With bated breath I kept rejoicing,

"Thank you friends, for these blessings!

 God has surely been good to me."

As night falls and this day comes to an end

I'm mindful of the Creator's grace.

"Thank you Divine Protector. You have walked with me throughout this year. Continue to be by my side and inspire us."

Amen

50th Wedding Anniversary

Oh! How life has been good to us

And has graced us with amazing gifts

What else could we ask?

Loving God, "We thank you!"

It's not only us you have touched.

It's our family, and friends who have walked with us.

They have comforted, and helped us along the way.

To all our anniversary well-wishers, "Thank you!"

You were with us on this journey with challenges

But as we encountered them we grew stronger

For such blessings, "We thank Our Creator!"

To honor this day on June 13, 2020

We light a candle of hope and look ahead

It's not just getting older,

But wiser in mind, body, and Spirit

Nor must we forget to thank our son Matthew

And daughter-in-law Shannon,

For being wonderful blessings in our lives

Plus all our relatives, who supported us

Let this candle continue to burn

Let us acknowledge the Divine of our lives,

The Supreme Being guiding us

And like radiant beauty we welcome

The golden flowers that have sprung from our garden

*"Omnipotent Creator, Thank you for guiding us these 50 years, and
continue to bless our marriage for as long as we shall live."*

Amen

Streams of Love

Universal Spirit you're Our Defender

And is present with us in all faiths

Be they Christian, Hinduism, Islam,

Confucianism, Daoism, or Shintoism

Whether you're monotheistic or polytheistic

Your glory reigns over all

So continue to guide us in righteousness

Let us learn to love our brothers and sisters

Wherever they live – in the East, West, North, South, or Middle East

Let us not look at their religion

The language they speak, nor the color of their skin

Remove from us the blinders so we're able to see all nationalities
    clearly

As European, Asian, or African

But let us look firstly at people's character

Based on the sound and ethical values of their faith

Let this be our simple prayer

By which we wish to foster the brotherhood and sisterhood

Of all men and women who live on planet earth

Hear our prayer, and walk with us where ever we go

Throughout this beautiful world with trees, mountains, valleys, plains, oceans, rivers with streams of love

Amen

"Universal Spirit, guide us to be instruments of peace throughout the length and breadth of planet earth."

Miracles of Summer

What a time to bask in the sunlight

Enjoying the breeze sweeping across the landscape

Hearing the birds chirping in trees

And taking a plunge in the ocean

Its summertime!

Everyone is out and around

Enjoying the scenery – having picnics,

Hiking and sailing

Just hop into a convertible

Take a trip to the countryside

That's blossoming with delight

Summer is one of warmest times of the year

Children sell lemonade on street corners

People buy ice-cold treats, and enjoy an ice-cream cone

Yes, its summer – a happy time in our lives

This season Our Eternal Essence graces us with abundance

And it's warm, often pleasant, and relaxing

It's the time when plants are flourishing with flowers and fruits

So just kick back and watch the Divine at work

"Glory is to our gracious God, who has blessed us with oceans, rivers, and sunlit streams of water.
Mountains, hills, flowering landscapes with roses and daisies, birds and brilliant sunlight are ready to greet us. Universal Essence, help us to enjoy these wonders as you reveal such miracles in summer."

Amen

Mother's Day Prayer

For Moms on Mother's Day

To all mothers, grandmothers, and great grandmothers

You're special in our eyes

You're the ones who bore the children of nations

You're the women who undertake the brunt of the responsibility in our homes

In nurturing, loving, and shaping us to become the people we are

You've dedicated your lives to the tasks of raising us to be the best

And you pursue these goals with an all-encompassing love

The Universal Spirit has blessed you with the "Special Gifts of Motherhood"

You walked with your children in confidence raising us in the world

So the Eternal Spirit has graced you with teaching us what's right from wrong

And to be assets to the societies in both great and small nations

You've raised children in every land of different faiths

Christians, Muslims, Buddhists, Hindus, and Daoists

Yet, although diverse, they live according to the Golden Rule

Yes, they are to "Do unto others as you would have them do unto you."

Great Spirit, you've gracefully blessed the mothers of our lands

And guided them to be the best parents

For such blessings husbands and children say,

"Thank Divine Protector for your loving blessings of our outstanding mothers from the bottom of our hearts."

Amen

Father's Day Prayer

Eternal Spirit guide our fathers

That they may always do

What's right in your sight!

Keep them safe

As they go about their daily lives

So that they may be at peace

Help them as parents to their children

And good husbands to their wives

Give them wisdom and understanding

To know what's best in troubling times

Comfort them and be with them

All the days of their lives

Great Spirit, you who makes no distinction

Of race, color, and creed

Be with the dads in every home

Help them to be good mentors in their families

Teach them how to accept criticism

When their efforts fall short

As parents, grand-dads, and great grand-dads

Bless and keep our dads always

Universal Spirit, walk with them

Talk with them

And guide them

To be good leaders in their families,

Communities and nation

"Eternal Essence by the grace of God, watch over dads. Lift them up to be the best dads, grand-dads, and great grand-dads they can be. For these blessings we pray."

Amen

On Labor Day

God thank you for the diversity

That has graced our lands

People have come from Europe,

Asia, Africa, and Latin America

Divine Essence we have evolved

From hunter-gatherers,

To farmers, builders,

Educators, warriors, and peacemakers

But behind our accomplishments

You have been our Guide

We are loving fathers and mothers

Raised families in communities,

And build nations

But it was through your grace

Your gifts have shaped our destiny

Eternal Spirit we have become a nation

Molded by your blessings

As Jews, Christians, Muslims,

Hindus, Taoists, and Secular Humanists

But still we are citizens

Not only of America, but the world

*"Divine Essence let freedom reign as we undertake our mission in life.
Guide and bless us as we strive for interdependence by the way we live."*

Amen

Joys of Christmas

Christ, a little babe was born in a manger

With Mother Mary and Father Joseph

So were animals keeping watch that memorable night

And that's the story of Christ's birth

Christ's birth nations celebrate on December 25th.

For it's on this day when Christmas trees

Are glowing with colorful lights

With presents on their branches

And many gifts lie beneath the trees

In the splendor of this season

Green wreaths with red and silver decorations

Adorn homes during these festivities

Christmas is a time to celebrate our Savior's birth

So let church bells ring and trumpets blast

For a King is born in Bethlehem

The world has been blessed with a Savior

There's an outpouring of love this season

People rejoice and the hope of the world are renewed

Many buy gifts for loved ones.

And children are joyful on Christmas morning

When Santa Claus comes bearing toys

Not even the poor and downtrodden are forgotten

For Christian believers make a special effort

To feed the poor and destitute with a Christmas dinner

That's how it is that churches are busy at this time of year

"Heavenly Father we give thanks for the joys of Christmas. And the celebrations, and good will that unite us all. Help us to live each day like its Christmas."

Amen

The Miracle of Life

Just imagine our chances of being born

In a world of over seven billion people

Living on five continents

Still you've come alive in this sea of possibilities

This is surely a miracle!

Imagine trillions of sperms

Vying for survival

In people, some white, black, yellow, and red

And no one could foresee

The eggs to which they will connect

And which ones will conceive

As a baby many of us have come into the world

Others as twins, triplets, or quads

But with our appearance only the Divine knows

What our birth and mission will be

Isn't this a miracle?

Often parents pray for a healthy baby

They ask the Universal Creator

To bless their family with such a wonderful gift

They are sure to nurture themselves

But their gift comes through nature

And these manifestations are the greatest miracle of all!

"Eternal Benefactor, continue to bless and direct our paths. Grant that with the birth of little ones, people would realize their dreams of having loving families."

Amen

Juneteenth Freedom Day

Over 200 cities in 49 states

And the District of Columbia recognize Juneteenth

Either as a state or ceremonial holiday or a day of observation

And activists are pushing Congress

To recognize June 19th as a national holiday

On June 19th, 1865, General Robert Granger

Issued a proclamation notifying black slaves

That they were free in Texas

This "Juneteenth Jamboree" grew in stature

And in many states it has become mainstream

The Anacostia Museum of the Smithsonian Institution

Has an exhibition Juneteenth '91, Freedom Revisited

Reading of the works of African American novelists

Like Ralph Ellison and Maya Angelou are popular

And singing of traditional songs like "Swing Low, Sweet Chariot"

And "Lift Every Voice and Sing" are sung at ceremonial gatherings

Celebrations on "Jubilee Day" include picnics, rodeos, and cookouts

Families have reunions, park parties,

Attend blues festivals

And there's a Miss Juneteenth contest

But all revelers never forget to have a Strawberry soda

The drink associated with these festivities

And for the more serious minded

There are lectures, exhibitions of African American culture

Accompanied by a voter registration drive

But to top it all everyone should participate in a barbecue cookout

The centerpiece of most Juneteenth celebrations

*"Divine Providence, bless these Juneteenth festivities on this notable
day of remembrance when African Americans began enjoying the fruits of
their freedom."*

Amen

Independence Day (U.S.A)

July 4th is an auspicious federal holiday.

It's unlike other holidays.

For the American Colonies were no longer subject to British rule.

This national day is a time for celebration.

Independence Day ushered in America's freedoms.

So let's commemorate this day of deliverance.

Let's fall on our knees in devotion to Almighty God.

And mark our nation's birth with pomp and parades.

Let fireworks explode and decorate the evening sky.

Americans celebrate with carnivals, fairs, and games.

It's time for reunions, ceremonies, and public events.

Independence Day began when the Second Continental Congress

Voted to approve the resolution for Independence proposed

By Richard Henry Lee of Virginia

Declaring the United States independent from Great Britain

From that time on its celebration

Was marked by gun salutes, speeches, music, and prayers

*"The Eternal Benefactor has continued to guide our nation.
Let's glorify this achievement. And let America's universal goal
perpetuate freedom for all – young, old, male, female, religious, and
non-religious with equanimity for all peoples – including LGBTQ+.
Regardless of their creed, color, and beliefs, let America stand as a
beacon of hope to the world."*

Amen

PART FOUR: SOCIAL GOALS

Acting with Actors

I'm an actor on the world's stage 24/7

But Sundays are special when I'm at church

Where I worship in the community

My church's friends perform like stars

Praying, doing penance, and making offerings

In humility to their loving God

Imagine what it feels like to have an acting part

In an ecumenical church

Chanting to hymns with organ music blasting

My feet shuffling with arms flaying to the beat

While moved by the Holy Spirit

Like worshipers it's exhilarating in the morning air

While belting out inspirational hymns

Parishioner are praising God and singing

And the priest is saying, "Give praise to God!"

Later, I hitched a ride home in a car

And through the bustling streets we rode

To my home where I live

But parishioners were only on the world's stage

Where thousands saw them on TV

At this Mass that Sunday morning

People are always actors some place

And you could usually see them on TV

"Loving God, make known your presence when we worship you at Church. Let our prayers reach out to heal all people throughout our communities."

Amen

Pursue Higher Goals

Make a pledge against sin, fallacies,

Idolatrous behavior, pride, and fear

By seeking God's friendship

And obeying his laws

Know God as freedom

For He grants us privileges

So continue doing good deeds

Even during the storms of life

Men and women are born

With a proclivity to sin

Many lives are marred by evil, pride,

And the display of selfishness

People don't act humbly

So let's change this behavior

To trusting in the Supreme Being

Listen to your conscience

Participate in communal prayer

In word and deed be sincere

And develop love in your heart

Towards those who have wronged you

People who are devoid of the power

To forgive, have no power to love

There lies some good in the worse of us

And some evil in the best of us

So love your enemies

Even though they might hate you

For through the Holy Spirit

Let's pursue the higher goals in our lives

"Divine Mediator, teach us to love all people. Help us to be trusting and sensitive even to our enemies."

Amen

Leaders' Role

Leaders must listen to their flock.

And hear what they are saying.

Everything doesn't work out as planned.

But there's often another point of view

To motivate people

So be sure to urge them on to higher levels

That's why it's essential to keep tabs

On the heartbeat of the group

In this way you'll learn more about them

Make decisions one step at a time,

Be sure to build on every success,

Never doubting that a group

Of individuals could change the world

Leaders must be people-oriented.

There's no room for tyrants or autocrats.

Even benevolent leaders who lead by whim

Cause harm to an organization

It's best not to be egocentric,

But work in the interest of the flock

For spirit-filled leaders often lead

With the interest of the group in mind

Leaders' role is to help people.

They must promote good relationships,

Be an example by doing away with methods,

That no longer works in the company

Their focus must be in stimulating growth,

And motivating others for their general good,

For results often come in small steps

*"Primal Essence, show organizations how to work harmoniously.
And guide workers to follow the democratic process."*

Amen

Journey in Life

How should people live their lives?

Firstly, people have to abandon feelings of being superior.

And endeavor to be humble in their daily walk

For they are all alike – created from the dust of the earth

So why fuss about who's greatest?

With growth comes independence

That calls for insight of their senses

What they see, feel, hear, taste, and smell

They should train their senses

Yes, people have to promote their well-being.

By the Eternal Spirit they learn the meaning of life.

They must listen to the yearnings of their souls.

These promptings they could only know through their senses

Some will discover they are introverts, others, extroverts.

"But what is their mission?"

Soon they are struck by the notion to love God.

Serve the Creator of the Universe

With all their heart, body, and soul,

And love their neighbors as themselves

This revelation comes with paying homage to the Almighty One

People should now dedicate their lives to be of service to humanity.

They ought to acknowledge their interdependence

As a cornerstone beneficial to society

*"Eternal Essence, help us with these goals to serve mankind.
Let us see that lives of interrelationships are the cornerstone of a
happy life."*

Amen

Be a Gift-Giver

Just don't accept gifts, but be a gift-giver

Our Divine Creator has honored us

With life itself – the greatest gift of all

We've been blessed with life's abundance

This ennobles us by providing many possibilities

Yes, we're born in unique families

To be nurtured as we grow

To be educated in the world's diversity in its Earth School

To take our rightful place among the peoples of the world

And we're in sync with nature's gifts

Flora, fauna, wind, water, and fire

We're truly blessed.

So how must we accept God's gifts?

That are shaping and guiding us through the paths of life

Firstly, let us praise the Omnipotent Creator.

It's the Eternal Spirit who supports us.

So we ought to give back to the world.

Therefore let us be of service to mankind.

Let our actions bring blessings to those we meet.

On rising in the morning greet everyone with a smile.

That's all it takes to send positive vibes out to the community.

You could do much more.

Why don't you reach out to the weak amongst us?

Help the depressed, poor, needy, and destitute.

Visit the sick in hospitals,

Greet believers in churches, temples, and mosques,

And on the highways, and byways

Serve the needy meals and comfort them

With the precious gifts our Divine Protector has given us.

"For all these blessings we pray – Universal Spirit help us! And be with us as we go out and come in when doing charitable works."

Amen

Live How You Like

Live how you like.

But do no harm.

And you'll be living the right way.

Yes! "The Universal Spirit is the Way, the Truth, and the Light!"

This motto captures the Spirit of living well.

How people behave has to do with how they think.

Daoism advised, "Go with the flow, and do what's natural. Be like water."

Confucius taught how to be virtuous;

And stressed the importance of social rituals

Christians would say, "Love God and your neighbor as yourself."

Jainism stated, "Protect all of life forms and do no injury."

But it's up to believers to find their path.

The religious might decide to be caregivers,

Dedicating their lives to the sick

Some might live a vegetarian lifestyle

For they respect the sanctity of animal life

Yet others might find a lifestyle of daily prayer

And devotion most helpful

While still others might feel that life was about service

To the poor, destitute, and handicap

But whatever is your mission, do no harm!

"Loving God, help us to understand the interrelationship of "yin" and "yang." Let us undertake a natural and holistic approach to life for the benefit of all creation. And Eternal Spirit, help us to follow a path where we do no harm."

Amen

World Day of Prayer

Divine Spirit and Creator of the Universe

Inspire the religious faiths of the world

To aspire to the Oneness of all beings,

And things, of which we're a part

Help us in our faith traditions

To express our beliefs in the true God

And let the religious commonalities

Of faiths resonate with their teachings

As we adore the Divinity of your Supreme Being

Guide the spirituality of leaders in Churches,

Temples and Synagogues

To be glowing lights to their believers,

And beacons of hope to all men and women,

By promoting hope, joy, and peace

So that people might reach out

To the homeless, poor, and broken-hearted

In our world racked with divisions

And Almighty God let us share our abundance

With all mankind wherever they might be

Whether in the slums of Africa, Asia,

Or Latin America,

Or, the urban centers of the Western World

Impacted by crime, violence, and racism

*"For these good gifts we pray. Protect your peoples around the world –
One God, now and forever more."*

Amen

Women in Society

Why should women be stuck in a world governed by men?

For a long time they were the caretakers

Who mainly cleaned the homes, raise the kids,

And did domestic chores,

Thus, they were stereotyped

Many males grew up seeing women as sexual objects

Even today the popular media focuses on feminine beauty

And women's sex appeal are played up

Some are portrayed as flaky, unstable, and emotional.

But independent women are sexier.

Today, they are building a new world

And coming into their own

Presently there are prominent women

In the arts, medicine, and science

Some hold top positions in the corporate world,

Military, sports, and politics

These outstanding women are visionaries,

Wonderful mothers, proven creators,

And renowned for their role models

But still they have a long way to go

In achieving equity – equal pay and respect

"Universal Spirit, help us to be respectful of women. And let us celebrate their achievements of those who have broken through the glass ceilings of this world."

Amen

Reusable Bags & Totes

When grocery shopping
Use reusable bags and totes
And do away with plastic bags
For these are harmful to the environment

Think about how bad plastic bags are
They are the culprits
That clog storm drains
Making their way into streams,
Lakes, rivers, and oceans
These plastic bags eventually disintegrate
Into small microplastics doing harm to birds, fishes,
And other species of marine life

Plastic bags are recyclable
But requires special equipment
They can't be placed in recyclable bins
But should go in special bins for plastics
More than 100-billion plastic bags are used in America
That go into landfills that aren't a good idea
So help save our planet by using reusable bags and totes

"Divine Spirit, help us when shopping. Let us act wisely by using reusable bags and totes."

Amen

Streams of Consciousness

Consciousness is like a river with running water.

This mindfulness stretches over a period of time

And makes us aware of ourselves and surroundings

It's the bedrock of our existence.

It's best to think about consciousness not only as a moving body of water.

But water that's always bubbling, and churning within us

Awareness usually begins as a small mountain stream.

That's only the beginning before people reach the "Ocean of Thought" – "Our Universal Mind."

This ubiquitous mind is the power of nature.

And symbolizes fertility – the growth and development of mindfulness

This consciousness guides and protects us on our journey through life.

Like moving water our consciousness is able to navigate impediments.

Consciousness symbolizes life itself.

It tells us whether we're on the right or wrong track.

And gradually or spontaneously reveals the beginning and end of all things.

It's inevitably the lifeblood of our existence

So be wise and nurture the well-being of the mind.

If our conscience is warped the entire world is out of sync.

So work on keep your mind healthy.

Serve people with mindfulness and pray,

"Eternal Spirit, help our mindfulness to be in harmony with nature. Inspire us to be good vehicles of your grace. And teach us to know ourselves better, and be of service to other sentient beings."

Amen

Be Wise about Power

Have a holy allegiance in life.

Embrace God's beauty

And live righteously.

With such a belief lies redemption

From sin, and salvation

So rid yourself of a hateful nature

Does power corrupt?

Power doesn't corrupt –

It's people who corrupt power.

So turn away from the corrupting

Nature of an evil heart

For its sin that led to the fall of humans

When actions betrayed their trust

So refine your heart with daily prayer

And not be blinded to the truth of the Word

Accept the expiation of your sins.

Continue to feed on your Savior's teachings

As you journey to glory

You'll surely face trials to test your character.

Cast aside lustful desires that weaken your soul.

Don't let conditions eat away

At the good inherent in you

For it's always right to remember

Transgressions of evil don't enthrone God.

So live like athletes for the living God

By persevering in faith

Be wise in using power.

"Loving God, help us to be wise about power. Grant us the grace to do what's always right in your sight."

Amen

Limitations of Prayer

Prayer isn't magic.

Much of life is predetermined.

The longest living land animals the bowhead whale could live for
200 years.

While the Mayfly only lives for 24 hours.

The oldest birds could live to 60 odd years.

These are parrots, vultures, albatrosses, and eagles.

With conservation efforts trees will live for thousands of years.

These are trees like Prometheus, Unnamed Great Basin Bristlecone
Pine, and the Jurupa Oak.

Another long lasting tree is the Sequoia of northern California and
Oregon

That could live up to 2700 years.

Prayer won't change the lifespan of flora and fauna.

Other conditions concern how species live.

Many species rarely approach their maximum age.

Some animals and birds die because of a high infant mortality rate.

Others die because of diseases, predators, and bad weather.

Lifespans are cut short because of habitat destruction

And competition for food and shelter

Religious believers must therefore know how and for what to pray.

There are some conditions that couldn't be changed.

But they should pray knowing that some conditions are the way they are.

Yes, we must pray for relief from the hazards that impact the living.

"Eternal Spirit, give us the insight concerning how to pray, and grant us relief from the hazards of earthly living."

Amen

The Sacred Elephant

For thousands of years

A majestic giant has graced our lands

It's the gigantic elephant known to all peoples

We find its symbol in India, China, Africa,

And even America

In India the elephant is known to Buddhists

And Hindus as the god Ganesha

As a defender and maintainer of good fortune

China, its symbol brings good luck, protection, and fertility

While in Africa the elephant is mighty

Because of its strength and power

But this gentle giant of mythology is patient,

Responsible, wise, clever, and smart

In the wild it cares for its herd and offspring

By nestling their young in loving ways

Let's elevate this admirable giant

To a greater place of prominence in our world

This animal's symbol continues to grace the world

With divine, pure, and secular gifts

Depicted in artworks, sculptures, and paintings

Indians pay their elephant-god Ganesha homage

The Chinese sing praises to this amazing animal

Africans view the elephant like a fortress in the jungle

And Americans embrace its symbol as a political party

Through the cartoonist Thomas Nast of Harper's Weekly magazine

*"Divine Essence, you have gifted us with an extraordinary animal.
We thank you for the elephant and all that it represents."*

Amen

Quest for Purity

In cultures water is used to commemorate the sacred

Symbolizing life, protection, and healing

But above all, different faiths use water for purification

Because it cleanses and washes away impurities

And is the objective of rituals in sacred ceremonies

Believers are at the mercy of water like the God they worship.

Buddhist monks used it for ceremonial rites of the dead.

Christians baptize with water and original sin is washed away.

Initiates are either immersed, have water poured over their heads, or
sprinkled.

Hindus seek cleansing in sacred rivers like Ganges, Yamuna, or
Godavari

For purification purposes, freeing themselves of pollutants,

And to attain Svarga (the paradise of Indra)

Some Muslims purify themselves before approaching God in
prayer.

Jews also practice rituals of washing.

Exodus tells the story of the Israelites' liberation,

Their journey through the Red Sea

And the drowning of Egyptians charioteers pursuing them

Water is also known to have other mystical qualities.

In different denominations it not only liberates,

But free believers from sin, and redeemed by God

To Christians the "living water" is Jesus Christ himself

Performing ritualistic rites in the Ganges

Dispels differences in the Indian caste system

That are often part of Hindu culture that Buddhism deplores

So every Hindu temple has a pond of some sort

For the rite of washing before entering the temple

"Eternal Spirit! Thank you for water that is used as the building block of life. And we are grateful for all its precious gifts to mankind."

Amen

Celebration of Wicca/
Pagan Litha Yule

Oh, where is the sun?

It's way up in the sky like a large wheel afire

Celts and Romans celebrate the turning of the wheel

That's a battle of light over darkness

Litha Yule, Midsummer Solstice, is the longest day of the year

The night is short, and it's a celebration of the sun's light

So let's us be like Wiccans

And glorify the power of the sun over darkness

Be sure to enjoy the day

Use diverse solar colors as you celebrate

Embrace the gifts of nature as summer begins

By enjoying the beauty of nature outdoors

Gather sunflowers from your garden

While in the park decorate a picnic table

Go swimming in the lake with the kids

And with the season's finest foods

Feast on a delicious barbeque outdoors

As night falls reflect on nature's beauty

It was a wonderful experience as the sun stood still in the sky

So ascend the hills and welcome its disappearance

Light bonfires and roll them down the hills

Then watch the balls of fire dissipate like the sun

On entering the waters in the valleys

Let people acknowledge

How much they appreciate the sun

That symbolizes new life, prosperity, and happiness

And light of an abundant harvest

The celebration ends at night with lighted sparklers

With enthusiastic crowds waving them saying,

"Goodbye my Benevolent Essence for such a glorious display"

*"Eternal Essence, thank you for the sun as it shines in all its glory.
Let us always celebrate its special present each year with an
outpouring of joy."*

Amen

PART FIVE: HOPE IN SUFFERING

Life Is Beautiful

Life is beautiful when people do what's right.

Then the fragrance of happiness

Will emanate to every corner of the world

That's when we are compassionate to the needs of others

And are bent on making life beautiful

People must embrace the gifts in all humanity.

Some might not be rich or born with halos

Yes, the poor might be thought of as the dregs of the earth

But still they embody the hope of a bright future

These rejected ones could be refugees,

The unfortunate and suffering

That are looking for a helping hand,

A home, job, and a place to rest their weary heads

Why can't we give these immigrants a break?

It's how people act that make them virtuous.

The love of God and others are all-encompassing

And involve showing good will

Life is beautiful when we could be of help to others.

"Merciful Provider you have made us all – rich and poor, immigrants, and refugees. Help us to be sensitive to the needs of others who are knocking at our doors. Let us remember that their lives are just as important as ours and that we should do everything in our power to help them to plant their feet on the ground. For these blessings we pray."

Amen

A Therapy Pet

A therapy pet could be a number of animals
Dogs, cats, llamas, miniature pigs, mini-horses, or birds
But some people choose dogs
They could be emotional-support dogs,
Therapy dogs, and certified service dogs

Why are these dogs necessary?
Dog owners attest to the benefits of having such pets
Because they lift their mood, relieve stress,
And help them recover from health problems
While in hospitals and mental institutions

Classrooms are also a good place too for such pets
Students benefit from them during physical exercise
Their interactions with these dogs lower their blood pressure
And having these pets around are stimulating
For they assist patients with pain management.

But there's a difference between a "therapy" and "service dog."
A therapy dog helps their clients physically and emotionally,
While a service dog helps people perform tasks
That they are unable to do themselves

"Divine Creator, help us to use these dogs in beneficial ways. Show us the best ways to work with such animals. And help us to treat these pets with love and kindness for what they do."

Amen

The Good in Suffering

Buddhists wish to escape suffering to achieve Nirvana.

But Christians embrace it.

And God tested the Israelites for 40 years in the wilderness.

The Father gives his Son as a suffering Christ, to save the world.

Christianity teaches suffering produces endurance,

And endurance character and character hope

So suffering is a form of learning

And believers should hold Christ as their model

For his yoke is easy and burden light

Christians should be patient in suffering and persevere in prayer.

Some saints prayed for suffering for redemptive purposes

Some civil rights leaders saw their goals could only be achieved

Through sacrifice, suffering, and struggle

So suffering should be embraced for moral development.

The best of us have known defeat, struggle, loss, and suffering.

Then there are people that are liberators that free people from the
bondage,

Poverty, deprivation, and discrimination

Nelson Mandela, a black South Africans became an anti-apartheid
  revolutionary.

So struggles could inspire people like him to rise to great heights

Such struggles result in victories for the equality for all.

*"Eternal Spirit, help people with their struggles to better the world.
Guide them to live and see their goals come to fruition."*

Amen

Good & Bad Luck

When good things happen people rejoice.

They exclaim, "Count your blessings!"

Many Christians believe the Holy Spirit

Is working in their lives

They embrace this goodness saying,

"I've been blessed and living right."

Good for them, and their beliefs!

But tragedy strikes!

A believer is stricken with cancer.

A family member dies in a car accident.

And these same believers say,

"I wasn't be living right."

But how true are such beliefs?

In every faith

Whether Christian, Islamic, Shintoism, or Daoism

Believers face similar problems.

Chance has something to do with their beliefs.

"It's based on fate," they say.

"Sometimes goodness comes to us.

At other times bad things happen."

Yet it appears with the laws of nature

Some people might always appear to be doing better than others

But stop and talk with believers

And you'll find out people all have struggles

Some are more debilitating than others

Maybe this is how the Eternal Spirit blesses us.

"It's therefore right to pray, "God help us to put our lives in perspective when it comes to chance!"

Amen

Make Lemonade

Who understands God?

God is the Source of Chance

It's through chance all things come into being.

People were born

They couldn't have planned their birth

Millions of sperms and eggs competed to become you

The erratic moods of creation is by chance

These are natural disasters.

No one knows for sure when one will strike

This might be an earthquake, volcano, hurricane, typhoon, or tsunami.

Yet experts act as though they know the reasons why disasters happen

But no one knows the workings of the Supreme Essence

With prayers people live in hope that everything will fall in place.

Some as they grow older are blessed with good health.

But as they continue to age the physical body breaks down.

As a result people suffer from chronic ailments

Like cancer, diabetes, chronic renal failure, dementia, multiple sclerosis, and heart disease

Some sufferers attribute these afflictions to bad luck

Not living right, or to hereditary factors

But these too are the normal cycle of life

There are some things people could do to ward off these inevitable problems

Yes, they could exercise, eat right, get a good night's sleep, and protect their minds from abuse

Yet with all they do no one knows when bad luck will strike

This could even be an unexpected fall or accident

The result of being in the wrong place at the wrong time

But how do people respond to the incidents that happen in their lives?

It's best to be thankful to the Universal Essence when they are blessed with good things

And as painful as their inevitable calamities might be

People ought to ask the Most Holy One for the grace to make lemonade with these lemons.

"Benevolent Creator, help us to live right. Let us see that chances in our lives are the result of your Divine plan."

Amen

A Balanced Life

Living is all about balance

It's the only way to live well

Because people are flawed

Aim for equilibrium

This is learning life's simple ways

Don't ever overdo, but weigh your options

It's what you do by how you live that matters

By being sure to embrace the basics

Eat balanced meals.

Every day walk 20-thousand steps

Get a good night's sleep

And challenge your mind

Be attuned to the Spiritual Force

Of the vast Universe

Do these fundamentals for healthy living

Remember to love and be loved

It's always good to be kind to people

For they are part of the human family

But who is your family?

They are also those you meet every day

On the highways and byways

The poor, homeless, and needy

Daily give praise to the Divine Creator

For all these blessings

For you'll be doing what's right

Just focus on being balanced

Help strangers by doing your heart's desire

That's how you'll be living a balanced life

In mind, body, and spirit

"Universal Spirit, help people pursue these simple steps for good health. Let them always remember to give thanks for your loving kindness."

Amen

God/Nature Fights Back

All life is interrelated and interdependent.

God/Nature is what we see, hear, touch, smell, and experience in diverse ways.

But still mankind has lots to learn about how nature works.

Mankind attempts to alter the face of nature for its convenience, health, and profit.

But nature has laws by which it functions that can't be broken without serious consequences.

Entrepreneurs have developed an industrial society, and are pouring tons of carbon emissions in the atmosphere.

For years there have been the uses of spraying on land and by air that have killed pests, an abundance of trees, wildlife, and animals alike.

These poisons have the effect of disrupting the metabolism in humans so many of us are dying from cancer.

Our world is armed with atomic bombs, and the radioactive fallout in some cases has poisoned our water supply.

Yet some leaders persist in making decisions that are harmful to human life.

So God/Nature has always fought back with the death, and deformities of millions and millions of species – animals, reptiles, birds, fishes, trees, and shrubs.

Many living species die immediately from the onslaught of poison, others linger, showing signs of malignancies, and there have even been noticeable effects on the weather.

Humankind is still to learn how to live with God/Nature in acceptable ways because God/Nature always retaliates with doomsday scenarios.

Living well with God/Nature has become an imperative that people can't afford to ignore.

It's for our own well-being, safety, health, and doing what's right for the preservation of future generations.

"God, help us to accept nature as an ally. Let us honor her gifts and preserve their benefits for future generations."

Amen

Healing in Life

Do you have constant headaches, low energy, and aching limbs?

Are you nervous with colds and sweaty palms?

Do you have clenched jaws and grind your teeth?

Do you suffer from palpitations and anxiety attacks?

Are you prone to violent outbursts?

Do you have a mental problem, an eating disorder, or are you obese?

Then you might be worn out with the demands of the world.

You could have a lack of appetite, addicted to alcohol, or nicotine.

Maybe you are pacing the floor, fidgeting, and unable to settle down.

With such a behavior you are unable to focus on your work.

You might even be suffering from some other chronic ailment.

But you just can't sleep at night, and have no sexual interest.

Your condition could be due to the rat race in the work place.

From childhood you were taught to be competitive.

"Be your best! The sky is the limit!"

You never knew it, but you were coerced to join the band of competitors.

Now you are running on overdrive and hooked on a computer.

You just can't find the time to relax and enjoy life.

But you could correct this negative course by embracing positive
changes.

Be sure to check with your doctor about your impending problems.

It will take is a change in your lifestyle before it's too late.

Make time to eat right, get a good night's sleep, relax, and exercise
to alleviate the stress.

*"God, help us with our health problems. Give us the insight to deal with
these problems so that we would be able to be healthy again. And grant
us the peace of mind to enjoy work."*

Amen

Partition Guyana?

Guyana is in turmoil

Since the Jagan-Burnham days

The nation was split

Between East Indians and Blacks

This is the legacy that has taken hold

And it makes no sense blaming the British

For that's the way of politics

Since this division in the 1950s

Voting in Guyana has always been suspicious

With East Indians and Blacks vying for power

International observers monitor the national elections

But still some results of the past were suspect along racial lines

American President Jimmy Carter headed one such team

The 2020 elections has again been marred

With accusations between the Afro-Granger and Indo-Jagdeo camps

There are accusations of rigging in Region 4

So once again there are upheavals with Blacks and East Indians

Where there was violence,

Innocent Guyanese terrorized, and some were killed

One great thing that has happened is Guyana now has an oil boom

With its population less than one million

There's a forecast that millions would be flowing into its economy

Why squander these resources with the country in turmoil?

It appears the best thing to do is to divide the country

Administratively and economically equally between the races

This will mean that Guyanese might still stand a chance to live in
peace

Will partition be the answer?

*"Gracious Creator, help Guyanese to work out their differences amicably.
Let its leaders show wisdom and good judgment in this country torn by
racial strife."*

Amen

LGBTQIA

The letters LGBTQIA

Means Lesbian, Gay, Bisexual, Transgender,

Queer or Questioning, Intersex, and Asexual or Allied

But why fuss over who they are?

In all ways they are alike

They come in the same colors –

Black, white, brown, yellow, and red

In races in every country

They live in our communities –

Towns, cities, villages, or the suburbs

Dwelling in homes, apartments, igloos, or huts

LGBTQIA eat the similar foods

German, Italian, Chinese, Spanish, African, or Native American

And worship in Churches, Mosques, Temples, or Synagogues

But their beliefs could differ based on who they are

Still they are just as devout and patriotic

Like those who are themselves straight

So let's stop looking only at differences

And honor our similarities

Let's reach out with love and compassion

To those who some people tend to demonize

For LGBTQIA are born the way they are

And although different they have similar beliefs

The Divine Protector in all his wisdom

Have made them the way they are

"Divine Protector, let's celebrate our diversity by giving thanks for your creativity. Help us to live in peace with all men and women in the world."

Amen

With Tears Help Us God!

O Merciful Father, God, and Divine Protector

Help us with the our tears

For the 12 killed and injured in Virginia Beach

Ease our pain and comfort us

To do everything in our power against such violence

We thank you for all the first responders

That risked their lives for the safety of countless others

We offer up prayers that people be secured in our city

That there will be protection for the innocent and vulnerable

That there will be peace in Virginia Beach

And that we'll have confidence in the good will of Virginians

Of diverse races, to be supporters of safety for all

Grant O Lord! Great Universal Spirit, that our sorrow will cease

As we mourn the loss of these precious citizens

And heal the wounds of the injured and abused

Give us the courage to continue to do business in our city

With fervor, and help us to prevent other such acts

Of crime from ever happening again

Eternal Spirit continue to nestle us under your wings

Always giving us the strength and will to oppose

What's wrong, and standing for what's right

Keep us safe, and help us to be true to you

In thoughts, word, and deed

Through Our Great and Everlasting Savior

Amen

A Pandemic Is Deadly

It could kill millions!

A pandemic spans the globe

Historically there were more flu pandemics

The flu pandemic of 1918 was the deadliest

It killed some 20 to 50 million people

Worldwide over 500 million were infected

Many victims of this influenza were healthy adults

A flu pandemic in the nineteenth century killed 1 million

In the twentieth century the Asian flu's death toll was 2 million

So in the 1950s and 1960s 3 million died

But during the twenty-first century HIV/AIDS struck

It was first said to be in the Democratic Republic of the Congo

And in its wake left 36 million deaths

Globally some 2.2 million to 1.6 million still die from this disease

But the thirteenth century witnessed the deadliest of all pandemics

This was the Black Death that swept through Europe, Africa, and
Asia

This disease was thought to originate in Asia

And took the form of a plague caused by infected rats living on
  merchant ships

The fleas of these rats caused the bacterium transported from port to
  port.

*"Merciful and Omnipotent God, help us in our battle with the
present outbreak of the COVID- 19 pandemic. Guide all sectors of
society worldwide in using their best judgment necessary to overcome
this scourge. Give wisdom and the scientific knowledge to our leaders for
keeping people safe during this crisis. We are help-mates and co-creators
in your Universe. God help those who help themselves."*

Amen

Chance: Key to Crisis

Chance! What a wonderful word.

It's the way to fight the coronavirus.

Keep your distance!

And I will keep mine!

Lock down and protect yourself!

It's best not to be caught in gatherings.

Protect yourself from this disease.

Assembling in groups could be deadly.

Where is God in our plight?

We shout, "Hear our prayer!

We can't stand it anymore!

Take this suffering away from us!"

"Act sensibly," God replied,

"Play your part.

You have to be smart to live.

It's all a part of life in the natural world."

When everything is settled

A new day will dawn

There will be peace and prosperity

And mankind will live in peace.

"Gracious Savior of the Universe, guide us safely through these confusing times. Comfort our hearts, soothe our souls, and make us realize that you hold the world in the palm of your hand. 'But how soon?' I cried. 'When will we gain relief from this scourge, and have your blessings again?'" There wasn't an answer. Then I thought I heard a gentle whisper, "This depends on us."

Amen

Dove of Healing

Had a dream while fast asleep

Of a white dove hovering overhead

While watching in amazement

I was struck that it was flying towards me

Fluttering it landed on my lap

What does this mean?

The world is in crisis over the coronavirus outbreak

I was stressing about all those who have died

And the many more suffering

With respiratory ailments and infecting others

Is there hope in these uncharted times?

Certainly there is!

A white dove symbolizes peace and tranquility

It is love, simplicity, and friendship

My dream was a vision

And a blessing from the Holy Spirit

Yes! The world will heal

Suffering will pass

And there will be normalcy again

"Omnipotent Spirit, give us the will by taking the steps necessary as people struggle with the coronavirus outbreak. Guide us to be mindful of the vulnerabilities this threat poses to our loved ones. And help us in our quest to heal the broken-hearted and find relief."

Amen

Christ Is Risen!

Christ is risen!

It's a brand new day in 2020.

Let's all play our part by supporting the "War on Poverty."

With Christ's resurrection comes hope.

So let the poor rejoice!

Let our poor brothers and sisters persevere in life.

Be kind to them whether they live in the Americas, Africa, Asia, or Latin America.

Do what you can to save a life wherever you could.

Such a life might well be a great gift to humanity.

For each human being is born with an unknown potential.

So be sure to nurture the underprivileged, and the outcast with love, food, and shelter.

The Risen Christ is an outstanding symbol to humanity.

Christians revere his eternal name.

Yes, Christ is risen!

A new day has dawn!

Let the rich, famous, and little people do what they can to celebrate this blessed day.

So pay attention to those that need help in your neighborhood.

Teach them to fish.

And remember to lend the poor a helping hand and be blessed.

*"Eternal Savior you're the source of all our needs. Help us to be generous
by sharing whatever we have with the poor. We're grateful for the hope
you brought to the world by rising from the dead."*
Happy Easter!

Amen

In Honor of Service Men and Women

On Memorial Day let us be mindful
Of the battles fought and won for freedom
Let us bow down and kiss the ground
Where the fallen were put to rest

By this way we honor them
For a job well done
They were the brave ones – men and women
That fought to defend the rights of nations
And paid the ultimate sacrifice
These precious souls live in our memories.

By the grace of God let us take heed
Of the devastation of wars inflict,
Countless sufferings, brutality, pain, and death
But what are people to gain from such miseries?

Let's pray that victories in foreign lands
Not only bring peace but prosperity
With goals that citizens live up to the supreme task
Of letting peace reign, and banishing wars from all lands

*"Divine Savior, for such ultimate sacrifice we pray, 'Eternal Spirit –
be with our resolve.'"*

Amen

National Symbolism in Fire

Fire is an emblem of divinity, political, and social unity

For millions of years with fire our ancestors kept warm

It protected them from being attacked by wild animals

Served as a meeting place for tribal communities

Where religious rites like chanting and telling stories were performed

Most importantly after a hunt hunters cooked their meals

Ancient traditions glorify fire

In the Hindu tradition the goddess Shiva

Destroyer, transformer, maintainer, and preserver is depicted as
dancing in a circle of fire

The Book of Exodus describes Moses's encounter with a burning
bush

Classical Greek mythology shows how Prometheus

The champion of mankind stole fire from the gods to give to humans

Acts of the Apostles reminded Christian believers

How the Holy Spirit appeared to the disciples as flames of fire

In ancient Persia and Rome fire played a prominent role

The Zoroastrian religion made use of fire, and clean water to
represent ritual purity

While priests tended the eternal fires on fire-altars

In the Roman religion Vestal was the Roman goddess of the hearth

Who was the protectorate

And were served by chaste Vestal Virgins

Today Paris burns a flame of national significance

It's known as The Eternal Flame at the Arc de Triomphe

John F. Kennedy's Eternal Flame symbolizes eternal life

While the flame at the War Memorial

Shows Americans' profound gratitude towards the remembrance

Of our dead service men and women

*"Almighty Creator, help us to understand more fully the usage of fire.
Let us be always blessed by the good things it signifies."*

Amen

Selected Bibliography

Albanese, Catherine L. 1990. Nature Religion in America. Chicago, IL: The University of Chicago Press.

Atran, Scott. 2002. In Gods We Trust: The Evolutionary Landscape of Religion. New York: Oxford University Press.

Barlow, Connie. 1997. Green Space Green Time: The Way of Science. New York: Springer Science + Business.

Boyer, Pascal. 2001. Religion Explained. New York: Basic Books.

Carson, Rachel. 1962. Silent Spring. New York: Houghton Mifflin Company.

Chaisson, Eric. 2007. Epic of Evolution. New York: Columbia University Press.

Crosby, Donald A. and Jerome A. Stone. 2018. The Routledge Handbook of Religious Naturalism. New York: Routledge & CRC Press.

__________. 2015. More Than Discourse: Symbolic Expressions of Naturalistic Faith. Albany, NY: State University of New York Press.

__________. 2008. *Living with Ambiguity: Religious Naturalism and the Menace of Evil*. Albany, NY: State University of New York Press.

__________. 2008. *The Thou of Nature: Religious Naturalism and Reverence for Sentient Life*. Albany, NY: State University of New York Press.

__________. 2002. *A Religion of Nature*. Albany, NY: State University of New York Press.

Dennet, Daniel C. 2006. *Breaking the Spell: Religion as a Natural Phenomenon*. New York: Viking.

Dowd, Michael. 2008. *Thank God for Evolution*. New York: Viking.

Ehrlich, Gretel. *John Muir Nature's Visionary*. Washington DC: National Geographic.

Emerson, Ralph Waldo. 2012. *Nature*. Charleston, SC: CreateSpace Independent Publishers.

Flinders, Tim. 2013. *John Muir Spiritual Writings*. Maryknoll, NY: Orbis Books.

Goodenough, Ursula. 2000. *Sacred Depths of Nature*. New York: Oxford University Press.

Guthrie, Stewart Elliot. 1993. *Faces in the Clouds: A New Theory of Religion*. Oxford, NY: Oxford University Press.

Haught, John. 2006. *Is Nature Enough?* New York: Cambridge University Press.

Hogue, Michael. 2010. The Promise of Religious Naturalism. Lanham, MD: Rowan & Littlefield Publishers, Inc.

Kaufman, Gordon. 2004. In the Beginning… Creativity. Minneapolis, MN: Augsburg Fortress.

Martinez, Nathan. 2015. Rise Like Lions: Language and The False Gods of Civilization. Charleston, SC: CreateSpace Independent Publishers.

Miller, James B. 2003. The Epic of Evolution: Science and Religion in Dialogue. New York: Pearson/Prentice Hall.

Miller, Kenneth R. 2008. Only a Theory: Evolution and the Battle for America's Soul. New York: Viking.

Nadler, Steven. 2011. A Book Forged In Hell. Princeton, NJ: Princeton University Press.

Norenzayan, Ara. 2013. Big Gods: How Religion Transformed Cooperation and Conflict. Princeton, NJ: Princeton University Press.

Raymo, Chet. 2008. When God Is Gone, Everything Is Holy: The Making of a Religious Naturalist. Notre Dame, IN: Sorin Books.

Rue, Loyal D. 2011. Nature Is Enough. Albany, NY: State University of New York Press.

__________. 2006. Religion Is Not About God. New Brunswick, NJ: Rutgers University Press.

__________. 2004. Amythia: Crisis in the Natural History of Western Culture. Tuscaloosa, AL: University of Alabama Press.

__________. 2000. *Everybody's Story: Wishing Up to the Epic of Evolution.* Albany, NY: State University of New York Press.

__________. 1994. *By the Grace of Guile.* Oxford, NY: Oxford University Press.

Ruse, Michael & Travis, Joseph. 2009. *Evolution: The First Four Billion Years.* Cambridge, MA: Belknap Press.

Russell, Sharman Apt. 2008. *Standing In The Light: My Life as a Pantheist.* New York: Basic Books.

Scott, Eugenie C. 2008. *Evolution vs. Creationism: An Introduction.* Berkeley, CA: University of California Press.

Stewart, John. 2000. *Evolution's Arrow: The Direction of Evolution and the Future of Humanity.* Canberra, Australia: The Chapman Press.

Swimme, Brian. 1992. *The Universe Story: From the Primordial Flaring Forth to the Ecozoic Era.* New York: HarperCollins Publishers.

Taylor, Bron. 2010. *Dark Green Religion: Nature Philosophy and the Planetary Future.* Berkeley, CA: University of California Press.

Appendix A

God in Different Religions

Religions present believers with diverse paths. These paths are concisely captured in the following faith traditions listed based on the number of adherents and importance as a faith based on their influence:

1. Christianity (2.2 billion) – Jesus Christ is the Son of God. God the Father and Holy Spirit complete the Trinity. This religion major problem is "sin." Christ came to earth, died, and resurrected to save mankind.

2. Islam (1.6 billion) – monotheistic with Allah as God, considers itself the true religion with Mohammed as its Prophet. Muslim beliefs are in the five pillars – repeating the creed, reciting prayers in Arabic, giving to the poor, fasting with certain abstentions from sunrise to sunset, and making a pilgrimage in one's lifetime to Mecca.

3. Nonbelievers (1.1billion) – atheists, agnostics, and people with no-faith tradition had its roots in fifth century B.C.E. Greek civilization and the Age of Enlightenment in the eighteenth century.

4. Hinduism (1 billion) – Brahman is the Ultimate Oneness. There is an infinite representation of gods and goddesses. Deities become incarnate in idols, temples, gurus, rivers, animals, etc. Hindus' quest is to become free from the law of karma – continuous rebirths.

5. Buddhism (500 million) – doesn't believe in God or gods. The big problem is escaping suffering, how to become Enlightened, and attaining freedom from the cycle of rebirth.

6. Chinese (394 million) – Confucianism (5–6 million) and Taoism (20 million) are major Chinese religions. Their other faith traditions are Buddhism and Shamanism. Confucian rituals formalized how Chinese should act in society. Daoism does the opposite and sees "the way" as being natural by going with the flow – practicing nonresistance.

7. African – Yoruba religion (100 million) of West Africa and its diaspora consist of a vast pantheon of superhuman beings known as orishas [adapted as Candomble (167, 363) in Brazil, and Santeria in Cuba (22,000 United States)] promoting believers' harmony with nature with divination rites, and some practices influenced by Christian traditions.

8. Sikhism (23 million) – Overcome the self. Align with the will of God, and become a "saint soldier," fighting for good. Sikhs believe in reincarnation until resolve karma and merge with God.

9. Judaism (14 million) – Abrahamic religion like Christianity and Islam that shared its influence of monotheism. Jewish teachings are based on the Books of the Old Testament and the Talmud.

10. Shinto (3–4 million) – polytheistic Japanese with "kami" worshiping ancestors, rain, wind, mountains, rivers, and trees, and fertility, etc. Buddhism and indigenous religions are also present.

11. Jainism (4 million) – polytheistic faith of Indian tradition, affirms the existence of all life forms, with beliefs in nonviolence.

12. Zoroastrianism (200,000) – Persian monotheistic and dualistic with "good" versus "bad," is believed to have shared this concept with Judaism.

"Universal Spirit, shine your light on all faith traditions and help believers find their rightful path."

Amen

Reference

The Big Religion Chart: Religion Facts
http://www.religionfacts.com/big-religion-chart

Appendix B

Well-Known Religious Naturalists

Ian Barbour (1923–2013), educator

Ralph Wendell Burhoe (1911–1997), interpreter of religion

Robert S. Corrington (b. 1950), philosopher

Donald A. Crosby (b. 1932), philosopher

Terrence Deacon (b. 1950), neuroanthropologist

Michael Dowd (b. 1958), Christian minister

Loren Eiseley (1907–1977), anthropologist, educator, and philosopher

Ursual Goodenough (b. 1943), biologist

Philip Hefner (b. 1932), theologian

Mordecai Kaplan (1881–1983), Jewish Rabbi, essayist, and educator

Stuart Kauffman (b. 1939), medical doctor, and theoretical biologist

Gordon D. Kaufman (1925–2011), theologian

C. Robert Mesle (b. 1950), theologian and educator

Karl E. Peters (b. 1939), educator and philosopher

Varadaraja V. Raman (b. 1932), Indian–American educator

Chet Raymo (b. 1936), writer and educator

Royal Rue (b. 1944), philosopher

George Santayana (1863–1952), philosopher, essayist, and poet

Jerome A. Stone (b. 1935), philosopher and theologian

Henry Nelson Wieman (1884–1975), philosopher and theologian

About the Author

For over 25 years Guyanese-born Erwin K. Thomas, Ph.D., was a professor and graduate director in International Journalism & Broadcasting at Norfolk State University, VA. He also taught at the University of Wisconsin, Milwaukee, and SUNY, Oswego, and has published nine books. Two were on the mass media (with co-editor Brown H. Carpenter), devotionals, an autobiography, and a novel. He is married to Mary Barta Thomas, and they are members of the Church of the Holy Apostles in Virginia Beach. VA. Their son Matthew lives with our daughter-in-law Shannon Mabry in Charlottesville, VA.

Website: https://www.bestprimalessence (Dfurstane)

Email: dfurstane@gmail.com